The Guide to Hawaiian-Style

Origami Charms

by Jodi Fukumoto

ISLAND HERITAGE

This book is dedicated

to my daughter,

Kiara

Table of Contents

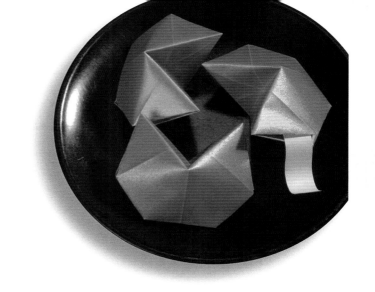

Foreword

Hawai'i is truly a beautiful place unlike any other in the world. Beyond the physical beauty of the land is the warmth and the friendliness of the peoples who live here. Those who encounter Hawai'i are blessed to discover the vast array of cultural traditions that come together to form the sentiment known as the Aloha Spirit. In this book, Jodi Fukumoto has artistically brought together many of the cultural symbols that characterize this spirit of giving of oneself.

It is also in the Aloha Spirit that Jodi shares her own talent of conceptualizing and creating origami. In this, her fourth origami book, Jodi s original work combines symbols of good luck and items unique to Hawai i with traditional Japanese origami to produce art unlike any other. Because many cultures affiliate certain coins with luck, it is fitting that many of Jodi s pieces artfully incorporate coins. Furthermore, she has designed several special papers to be used in these pieces to help her work come alive.

Jodi s beautiful creations are an amalgam of objects that represent the cultural melting pot that is Hawai'i. In this book, one will sample many cultural flavors and experience the Aloha Spirit firsthand.

Jessica Murakami

Acknowledgments

Mahalo nui to my mother, Barbara Fukumoto, for making this book possible;
to my niece, Jessica Murakami, for writing a beautiful and expressive foreword;
to Karen Harunaga, the librarian at Hongwangi Mission School,
for her assistance on Japanese subjects;
to Island Heritage for all that they do and do so well;

and

to my daughter Kiara—
thank you for taking the time to really look
at the hundred things I put before you and
for answering the hundred questions asked
with the wonderful observations
of both an artist and a child.

Introduction to Origami Charms

The origami charms in this book, which range in subject matter, all fall under the theme of Hawai'i. Although some of the figures, or models, originated in other countries, they are very much a part of Hawai'i's diverse cultural heritage. Many of the models are recognized as images of good fortune, several represent holidays, while others simply say Hawai'i.

All of the models, with the exception of the Fortune Cookie, are coin holders. Each model has a pocket or compartment in which to place a coin. Model sizes are based upon the American Sacagawea gold dollar. This beautiful and unique coin appears to have more than just monetary worth. Its design and golden color have made it a cherished and possibly lucky keepsake. The gold dollar is seen in most of the examples.

The models in this book were contrived around the concept of giving, whether as a single token of luck or as a circle of many wishes in the form of a lei. It is in the giving, behind your feelings and intentions, that these models actually become charms.

The primary use for the coin-filled charms is as lei charms. Most are best utilized in lei made from lei netting or tubing; a few may be strung. Several of the models are reinforced with extra folded layers, which make them more durable for wearing.

In terms of lei charms, choice of paper matters. For instance, models created from foil origami paper are nice but definitely not very strong, especially those models that are three-dimensional. Hence, it follows that you could use paper slightly thicker than the norm to strengthen the structure of certain models. Please read the model information that heads the instructions of each. Note paper size, especially any custom paper size, and finished model size. A recommended custom paper size, which must be cut, will create a model that is of a more suitable size for lei making.

Another great use for origami charms is to add them to party or school goody bags. Again, use your judgment in selecting models that won t crumple under pressure.

Many three-dimensional models can be presented in two-dimensional form. (Check individual model information for model dimension.) In most cases, only little subtleties are lost, but then again, it is often the little subtleties that make a model endearing. So overall, three-dimensional models are best in three-dimensional form. Two-dimensional charms may be useful for greeting cards, letters, and thank you notes. For more ideas and uses, see photographs of model examples.

Model Care

To insure that your gift doesn t unfold in the slightest upon receiving:
- Use glue to lightly tack together layers that tend to separate. Use the least amount of glue possible. The idea is to keep the appearance of individual layers and not to completely join them together as one.
- If you have folded your gift in advance, use paper clips to hold and continue to set certain folds until you are ready to present your model.
- Store models in airtight containers or plastic bags.
- Store two-dimensional models without coins between the pages of a heavy book.

Stringing Lei

A. The easiest way to string origami charms into lei is to use lei netting or poly tubing, which can be found at most craft or general mechandise stores. Lei netting, which is tubular, stretches and conforms around any shape. It is available in many colors. Poly tubing is available in widths of 2, 2.5, and 3 inches. It is sold by the roll or by the yard in different thicknesses. It is also available in packages of precut lengths.

Poly tubing in the 2-inch width is recommended for lei consisting of only the Coin Frame, Dolphin, or Shave Ice. The *Maneki Neko* and Girl's Day Doll will also fit into this width, or you could use the next size. Use poly tubing in the 2.5-inch width for all other models. If you are purchasing poly tubing specifically for the Chinese Lion, Rooster, or Lucky *Lūʻau* Pig select the 3-inch width size. Please remember that these suggestions are based on models created from the recommended paper sizes.

Poly tubing is available in several tints and in clear. The tinted tubing, which is sold mainly in 2- or 3-inch widths, is somewhat dark and may obscure the colors and detail of your models. Clear is recommended. A strip of tinted tubing may be placed within the clear tubing and used as background color. Cellophane or tissue can also be used in this manner. Or create your own tubing or wrap from cellophane. Be sure to choose lightly tinted cellophane that is easy to see through.

In addition, you will need ribbon or raffia to section off the models in the tubing. Choose ribbon that does not fray. You can also use other items for this task, including little hair clips or decorated hair ties, beads, little silk or ribbon flowers (preferably with soft wire stems), or shells. Search craft stores for ideas.

B. To create a lei for the average adult, cut a length of tubing approximately 4.5 to 5 feet long. For a child, cut a length 3 to 3.5 feet long. Cut your ribbon to desired lengths. Fold the tubing in half to find its center. Place a model in the center and tie off the tubing on both ends of the model. Place the rest of the models into the tubing. Remember to position the models correctly on each side of the center model so that none of the models are upside-down when the ends of the tubing are tied together. Section off each model by tying the tubing with pieces of ribbon. You may wish to intersperse the models with candies or little gifts.

It is also possible to actually string several of the models into lei. Use thick thread, yarn, or very fine decorative cord. Follow the same procedure used to string coin frames, which is shown at the end of the instructions of the Coin Frame. Use two lengths of cord if you want to prevent the models from spinning and revealing their other sides. Unless you have a very long needle, such as a doll-making needle, you may need to unfold certain models in order to sew them from end to end. It is also necessary to glue pertaining layers or sides of a model together to secure the coin in place.

Many of the models can also be fastened onto flower or candy lei or goody bags with thread, yarn, or very thin cord. To accomplish this, place a strip of clear tape on the back of your model. Sew one large running stitch 0.5 to 1 inch long through the tape and back layer(s) of the model. Cut your thread to sufficient length. The tape will prevent the thread from tearing your model when you tie it onto your lei or tie a goody bag closed. If you don t want the tape to show, place it on the inside of the back layers of your model.

Part One: How to Use This Book

A. Supplies

1. Using the Enclosed Paper

This book includes paper specially designed for the *Maneki Neko*, Boy's Day Carp, Girl's Day Doll, Chinese Lion, Shave Ice, and Pineapple. Each paper design, when folded properly, creates the same model seen in the book. The special paper is located in a pocket on the inside of the back cover. Please note that the above-mentioned models may also be folded from plain paper.

How to use the enclosed paper:

• Select the correct paper by design or by label. Two sheets of each design are offered.
• Use the printed X on your paper to correctly position it as shown in the initial steps of the model s instructions.
• Each instructional line and point on your paper is labeled with the number of the corresponding instructional step. Match step numbers. The line on your paper may not always be the same color as the line in the instruction step.
• Not all steps have corresponding instructional lines printed on your paper. An asterisk will precede a step s number or letter to inform you there is a corresponding line on your paper.
• Printed center lines, which enhance creases made by folding your paper in half, are *not* labeled.
• Folds are made exactly on fold lines and not on guide lines. Guide lines are provided as reference points. See example below:

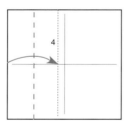 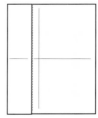

*4. Fold edge to printed line 4.

2. Origami Paper

To make the charms, you will need perfectly square sheets of thin paper, such as origami paper. If you intend to use your models as coin holders, the paper dimensions listed below are recommended for the models specified. These dimensions are based on creating a model of suitable size in which to present the American Sacagawea gold dollar (you may substitute a Susan B. Anthony dollar or, unless otherwise noted, an American quarter). Origami paper sizes are stated in centimeters as printed on most origami paper packages. An equivalent size in inches is provided for those who wish to cut their own paper. Please read the model information that heads the instructions of each model for suggested types of paper and custom paper sizes. A few models recommend a custom paper size, which must be cut, to create models for lei.

• **Origami paper 15 X 15 cm,** or paper 6 inches square, can be used to fold most of the charms in this book. This standard origami paper size is the most popular and is available in a large assortment of prints and color patterns, as well as in multicolored packs.

• **Origami paper 17.5 X 17.5 cm,** or paper 7 inches square, is required to fold the Rooster. You may also use this size to fold the Fortune Cookie. Paper of this dimension is sold in multicolored packs and in a limited assortment of designs. Use origami paper 15 X 15 cm to fold models of the Rooster for quarters.

• **Origami paper 11 X 11 cm,** or paper 4.25 inches square, is needed to fold the Dolphin. This paper size is mainly found in single color packs of paper or paper-backed foil. Models for quarters require paper 4 inches square.

• **Origami paper 7.5 X 7.5 cm,** or paper 2.75 inches square, is required to fold Coin Frames. This paper size is available in color patterns, a few prints, and multicolored packs. Use paper 2.5 inches square to frame quarters.

You can purchase origami paper in art, craft, and hobby supply stores or at stores that specialize in Japanese or Asian merchandise. Hawaiian-Style Origami Paper (paper with Hawaiian prints used in this book), 6 inches square, can be found wherever this book is sold or through www.islandheritage.com.

3. Other Supplies
You may also wish to have on hand: paper clips, glue, tape and/or double-stick tape, quality toothpicks, and a tapered chopstick or similar item. Read the model information that heads the instructions of each model for any specific needs. Supplies for lei making are described in the "Stringing Lei" section.

To measure and cut your own paper or to trim origami paper to a desired dimension, you will need at minimum: a ruler, a pencil, and a pair of scissors. If you feel that this is not sufficient for your needs, I recommend using a quilting square, an X-acto Knife with a number 11 blade, and a cutting mat. A quilting square is a clear acrylic template with precise grid markings that allow you to accurately measure squares of many sizes. You can find quilting squares of various sizes and brands at craft stores and sewing centers. Ask the salesperson for recommendations and on how to use the grid pattern to measure smaller squares. With an X-acto Knife and cutting mat, you can quickly cut squares of all sizes without marking your paper. These items are available at craft and art supply stores.

B. The Fundamentals of Origami

1. Steps

a. Steps are numbered. Follow the instructions step-by-step. Do not skip any steps.

b. Each step contains a diagram and written instructions that show and tell you what to do. To help understand an instruction, look at the next step to see the result.

c. An intermediate step may also follow an instruction to show how to accomplish the required fold. An intermediate step is labeled with a number and a lowercase letter.

2. Drawings

a. Instructional drawings do not always depict edges and folds perfectly aligned as they actually should be. This is in order to show existing folds and layers. In the example given under Precision , the left side is properly aligned while the right side is shown askew, exhibiting folds and layers.

b. Drawings may be enlarged to clarify instructions. Significant enlargements are noted by the letter *E*.

c. When a section of a drawing is outlined with a box, only that section is magnified and shown in the following steps.

3. Precision

a. Take your time and be as precise as possible. Press hard to make sharp creases.

b. Match and fold all pertinent edges, creases, and points exactly together.

c. Align center lines when they pertain to a fold. A center line is a crease that runs through the center of your paper, model, or a section thereof.

 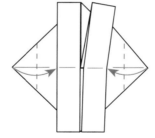

Align center lines to fold accurately.

C. The Key to Lines, Folds, and Arrows

1. Lines

———————————— **Edge**

———————————— **Crease**

·· **Unseen Edge / Unseen Fold / Guide**

– – – – – – – – – – **Fold**

–·–·–·–·–·–·–·– **Mtn. Fold**
(mountain fold)

Edge lines and crease lines, which are usually **black** are occasionally highlighted with color.
The color of all other lines may vary between red, blue, and **black**.

2. Simple Folds and Arrows

Arrows vary in color and size. Fold arrows also greatly vary in shape.

Fold
Fold section in front.

Unfold
Unfold section.

Fold; unfold
Make a crease.

 **Mtn. fold**
(mountain fold)
Fold section behind.

To Mtn. fold:
Turn paper over. Fold edge
to crease. *Turn paper
back over.*

 **Lift**
Lift flap
perpendicular. *To Lift:*
Fold to establish
crease if needed,
then lift flap at
right angle.

Indicates an important
edge, crease, or point (pt.)

Open layers, sides, or
model **here**

 Press or pinch here

Push here or push in

 Turn paper / model over in direction of arrow

 Fold in-between layers
(see inside reverse fold)

3. Combination Folds

A combination fold combines two or more folds into a single step. These folds are made in a specific order, referred to as a folding procedure. The folding procedure is listed for all combination folds, as they are applied in the model instructions. These include the inside reverse fold, outside reverse fold, rabbit ear fold, petal fold, squash fold, pleat fold, and sink fold.

The inside reverse fold, the most common combination fold, is explained here in greater detail to help you accomplish it accurately.

Inside Reverse Fold

Example:

Inside reverse fold corner.
1. Establish creases: Fold corner to center; unfold.
2. Open sides to fold corner in on creases.

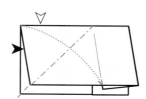

To inside reverse fold:

1. To establish creases, use the inside reverse fold arrow ·······➤ to show you where to fold an edge or pt. Align edges exactly and keep aligned as you fold corner to edge as shown; unfold.

Note: It can be difficult to accurately crease two layers at once. Minor adjustments can be easily made in the steps that follow.

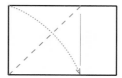

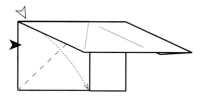

2. Open ➤ sides as shown.
3. To fold corner in on creases, push ▷ on edge to fold corner in on back crease first.

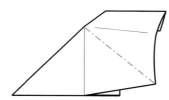

Note: *Edge is temporarily a crease. Pt. comes to exact pt. and edges match perfectly.*

4. Mtn. fold crease, pinching sides together to create a flap. Make a precise pt. Match edges.

5. Fold flap over to complete fold.

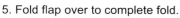

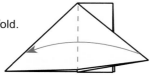

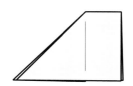

D. Color Coding

The colors red and blue are used to highlight instructional arrows and lines for the following purposes:

- To easily distinguish fold arrows and lines from edges and creases.

- To correlate the different arrows and lines of a diagram with the written instructions in folds that have more than one instructional arrow and/or line, such as the combination fold below. The colors also designate the order in which the folds are made. In general: red before blue; blue before **black**.

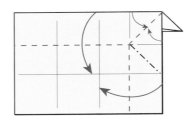

Rabbit ear fold flap.
1. Fold corner in half.
2. Refold edges in on creases.
3. Mtn. fold is made by folding flap down.

As seen, employing different colors makes it possible to easily explain combination folds in a model's instructions.

- To clearly define on a diagram unrelated instructions of a two-part step.
  As a rule, A is red and B is blue.

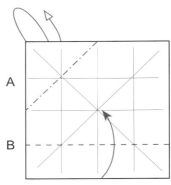

A. Mtn. fold corner pt. behind to center. Unfold.
B. Fold edge to center.

For the few instructions with three parts, **black** is used as the third color.

- To identify notable edges and creases and to correlate them with the written instructions. See example under "Precision" on page 10.

Part Two: Origami Charms

Maneki Neko (Good Fortune Cat)

The maneki neko, *or beckoning cat, is a beloved icon adopted from Japan. It is displayed as a ceramic figurine in most local business establishments and in many island homes as well. A white or gold* maneki neko *beckons good fortune with a raised right paw. A* neko *with a raised left paw welcomes customers or guests. And a black* neko *summons good health.*

Use the specially designed *Neko* paper, or origami paper 15 X 15 cm. The *Maneki Neko* is a two-dimensional model, 1.5 X 2.5 inches. **Note:** The following instructions are for use with both the special *Neko* paper and plain paper. Separate instructions are clearly labeled **Neko** Paper or **Plain Paper**. Shared instructions are not labeled. See "Using the Enclosed Paper" on page 8.

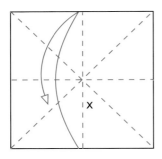

1. Begin with the desired side down or place X on **Neko Paper** as shown. Fold in half; unfold. Repeat.

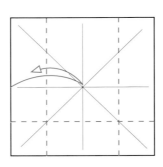

2. Fold and unfold each edge to center.

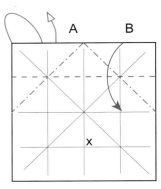

3.
A. Mtn. fold top corners behind to center. Unfold.
B. Fold edge to center.

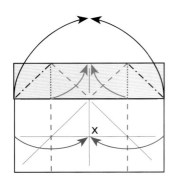

*4. On both sides and on creases: Fold edge pt. to center. Fold side in. **Mtn. fold** corner in half.

5.
*Neko Paper: Fold edge to printed line. **Unfold.**
Plain Paper: Determine or estimate reference pt. shown. Fold edge to pt. **Unfold.**

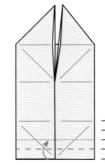

6. Fold edges to center.

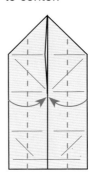

*7.
A. Mtn. fold corners behind to crease as seen on right. Unfold.
B. Unfold sides.

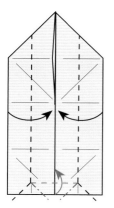

8a.

*8. On creases:
Fold midsection of edge up. (See 8a.)
Refold sides in.

A

B

Note: See step 14 for front view of result.

*9.
A. Fold edge of flap out.
B. Fold pt. of flap to edge.

*10.
A. Mtn. fold edge behind to first folded edge. See back view.
B. Mtn. fold corner pt. to edge.

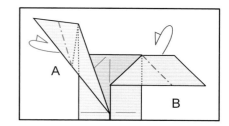

A

B

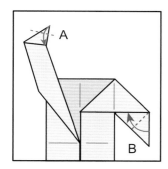

A

B

11.
A. Fold very tip under edge.
*B. Fold edge to edge.

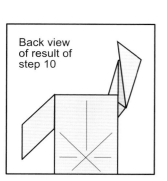

Back view of result of step 10

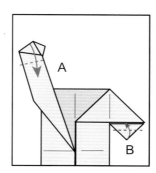

A

B

12.
A. Fold down at an angle.
*B. Fold pt. to edge.

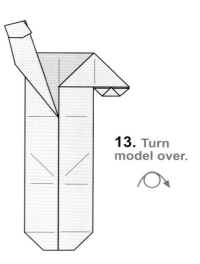

13. Turn model over.

Rotate model as shown.

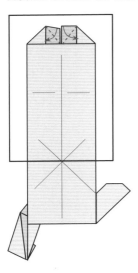

14. On both sides: Fold edge under edge just enough to hold it in place.

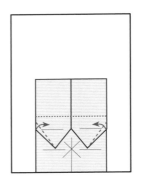

*15. Fold section down on crease.

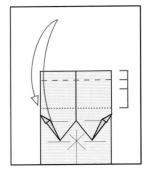

*16.
Fold edges of ears in.
Plain Paper: Note hidden edge.

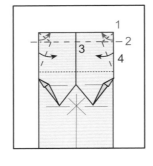

17.
*Neko Paper: Fold head up. Unfold.
Plain Paper: Fold head up. Note hidden edge. Unfold.

18. On both sides:
Fold section of edge to edge, up to crease, folding head back up on crease 3. Fold sides of head in.
Note: See finished model for front view of result.

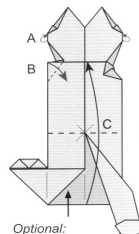

19.
A. Slightly curl edges to round sides of head.
*B. Fold down corners as seen on right.
*C. Fold edge to edge on crease.

Optional: To hide coin, place it under flap after 19C.

20.
A. Mtn. fold leg behind.
B. Fold down corner.
Turn model over.
C. Hook raised paw on head.

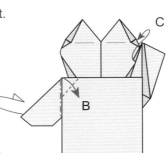

Tape coin with double-stick tape under paw as shown.

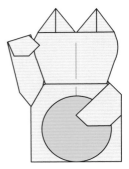

Boy's Day Carp

Koi nobori, *or carp streamers, are proudly flown on Boy's Day, May 5. This borrowed Japanese tradition honors sons and all boys. The carp, attributed with strength, determination, and long life, symbolizes masculinity.*

Use the specially designed Carp paper, or origami paper 15 X 15 cm. The Boy's Day Carp is a three-dimensional model, 1.5 X 4.5 inches. **Note:** The following instructions are for use with both the special Carp paper and plain paper. Separate instructions are clearly labeled **Carp Paper** or **Plain Paper**. Shared instructions are not labeled. See "Using the Enclosed Paper" on page 8.

1. Begin with the desired side or carp design down. Fold in half; unfold. Repeat.

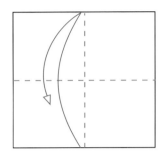

2. Fold each corner to center.

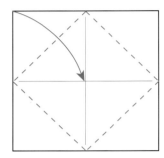

3.
Carp Paper: Place X as shown. Skip step A.
B. Align pt. on line 3B. Press finger-width crease. Unfold.
Plain Paper:
A. Align pt. on center. Press finger-width crease. Unfold.
B. Align pt. on crease. Press finger-width crease. Unfold.

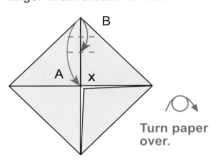

Turn paper over.

4. Fold pt. to crease. Unfold. **Turn paper over.**

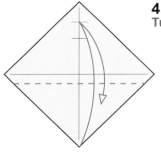

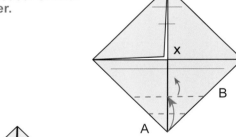

***6.**
A. Fold pt. to crease.
B. Refold flap up.

***5.** Fold pt. to center. Unfold.

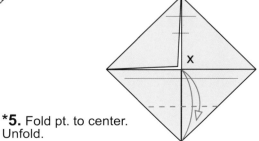

7.
*A. Fold edge to edge.
Carp Paper: Skip 7B.
B. Fold pt. to midpoint between creases. **Unfold.**

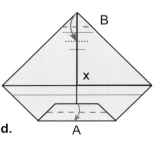

*8. Fold edges to crease.

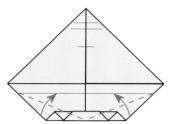

9. Mtn. fold corner pts. behind to center. Align pts. on crease.

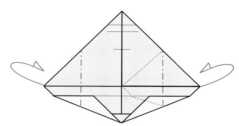

*10. Fold sides in between pts.

E

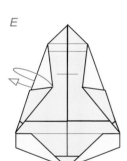

Optional: Steps 11 and 12 create a pocket used to lock the sides together. You may choose to skip these steps and to later glue the sides together.

11. Mtn. fold left section behind on same crease. Unfold.

*12. Sink fold section on creases.
1. Start with larger fold. Partially open layers.
2. Push pt. in on creases.
3. Push to invert remaining edge on left.

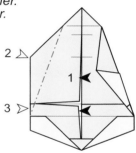

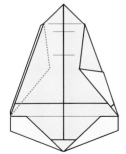

Note outline of pocket between layers.

13. Turn model over.

*14.
A. Fold edge to edge on indicated pt.
B. Fold edge to edge.

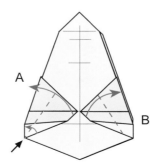

*15. On both sides: Open layers. Push edge in to inside reverse corner.

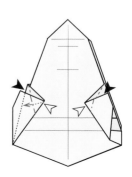

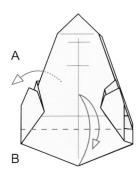

A

B

Note: Skip steps 16A and 19A if you plan to glue sides together.

16.
A. Unfold flap from behind.
B. Reestablish crease. Unfold.
Turn model over.

17. Rotate model as shown.
A. Lift edges and small flaps near pt. Leave indicated corners flat.
B. Fold sides together.

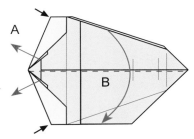

A

B

18.
A. Insert finger into head to round sides from the inside. Leave indicated lower corners flat.
B. Pinch head and fold up on crease. Set fold from inside.

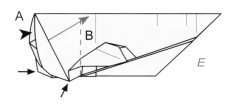

A
B
E

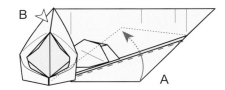

B

A

19.
A. Fold flap into inside pocket.
B. Push on top edge of head to widen to desired width.

Insert coin in mouth behind small flaps.
Fold flaps down to hold coin in place.

20.
A. Symmetrically fold edges of mouth down.
Optional:
B. Splay back fin to prop model up.
C. Insert pencil through tail end. Gently squeeze together top and bottom edges of body to round open sides. Remove

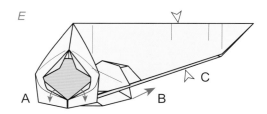

E

A
B
C

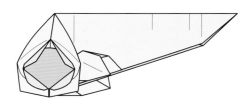

Girl's Day Doll

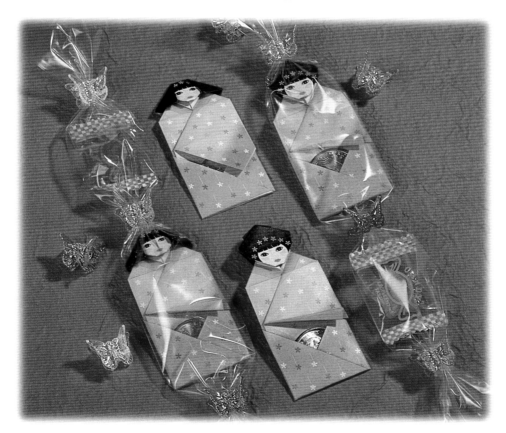

*Girl's Day, celebrated in Japan, is quietly observed in Hawai'i.
Beautiful Japanese dolls are displayed on this special day for girls.
Girl's Day falls on the third day of the third month of the year.*

Use the specially designed Girl's Day Doll paper, or origami paper 15 X 15 cm. The Girl's Day Doll is a two-dimensional model, 1.5 X 3.5 inches. **Note:** The following instructions are for use with both the Doll paper and plain paper. Separate instructions are clearly labeled **Doll Paper** or **Plain Paper**. Shared instructions are not labeled. The Girl's Day Doll instructions offer two variations of hairstyles and an optional fan design. Glue is recommended. See "Using the Enclosed Paper" on page 8.

1. Begin with desired side down or place X on **Doll Paper** as shown. Fold in half; unfold. Repeat.

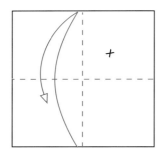

2. Fold and unfold edges to center. **Turn paper over.**

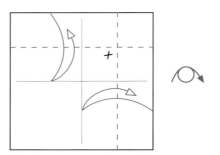

3. Fold corner to center; unfold.

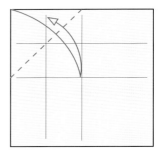

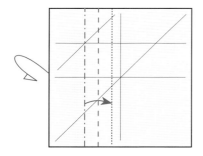

*4.
Doll Paper: Mtn. fold crease. Fold new edge to printed line 4. (See 4a.) **Unfold.**
Plain Paper: Proceed to additional steps A through E.

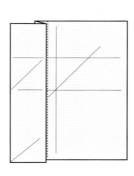

*4a.

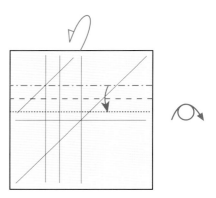

*5.
Doll Paper: Mtn. fold crease. Fold new edge to printed line 5. **Unfold.**
Turn paper over.
Proceed to step *6.

Plain Paper: The following additional steps are required. Steps B through E create a grid pattern in the center of your paper as seen in step 4 below. The lines and pts. on the grid are used for reference pts. for future folds. The grid is not visible in the finished model.

A. With desired side down, place paper as shown. Fold in half. Unfold. Repeat.

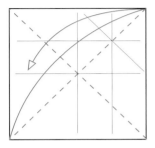

B. Fold in half.

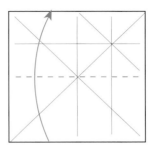

C. Fold in half.

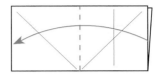

Steps D and E:
Align edge on crease.
Fold only to make crease as shown. Unfold.
Repeat on adjacent edge.

4. Unfold completely with desired side up. Mtn. fold on crease. Fold new edge along side of center square. (See 4a.) Unfold.

4a.

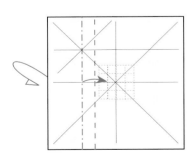

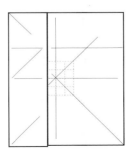

5. Mtn. fold on crease. Fold new edge to crease. Unfold. Turn paper over.

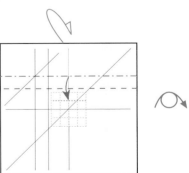

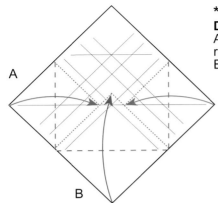

*6.
Doll Paper: Rotate paper as shown.
A. Fold side pts. in to
respective pts. 6A.
B. Fold bottom pt. up to pt. 6B.

6.
**Plain Paper: Rotate paper
as shown.**
A. Fold side pts. in to
respective pts. of center
square.
B. Fold bottom pt. up to top
pt. of center square.

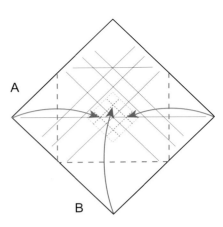

*7. On creases:
Fold edge pts. in
to center.

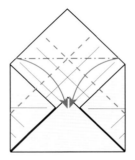

E

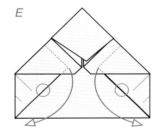

8. Pull out corners.

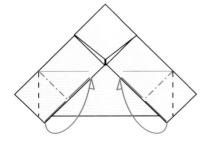

*9. On both sides:
On crease: Mtn. fold corner inside
under flap. Completely match edges
of new flap. Fold new flap down.

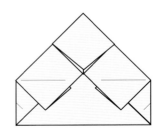

Before proceeding, choose a hairstyle
for your doll. Hairstyle 2 requires
additional steps.

1

2

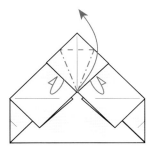

Hairstyle 2

Petal fold.
1. **Doll Paper:** Fold to establish center line; unfold.
2. Establish creases: fold edges to center. Unfold.
*3. Fold pt. up between crease pts. Fold edges in on creases. Gently stretch to align edges on center.

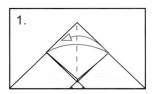

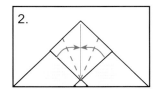

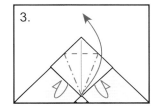

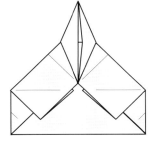

Hairstyle 2 is completed in later steps. Continue with instructions, which depict Hairstyle 1.

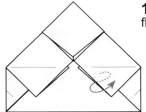

10. Lift right edge of center flap to overlap right flap.

11. Turn model over.

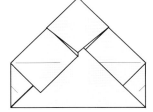

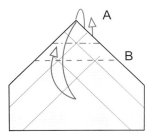

*12.
Doll Paper:
A. Mtn. fold pt. behind. Unfold.
B. Without folding hair flap behind, fold pt. to pt. 12B. Unfold.

*13.
Doll Paper:
Steps A and B:
Without folding hair flap behind, fold sides in.

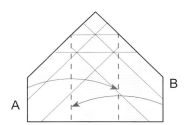

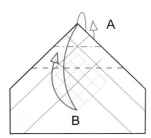

12.
Plain Paper:
A. Mtn. fold pt. behind on intersection pt. of creases. Unfold.
B. Without folding hair flap behind, fold pt. down to pt. of grid. Unfold.

13.
Plain Paper: Folds sides in, left side first.
Note:
1. Do not fold hair flap behind.
2. Match all bottom edges.
3. Use initial reference creases as guides.

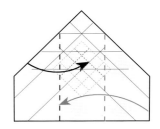

E

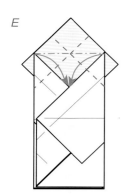

*14. On creases:
Fold edge pts. in to center. Flatten head flap down and set folds.

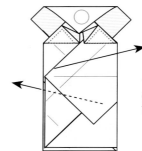

15. Gently hold head flap down. Lift sides to free trapped paper

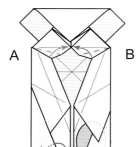

A   B

Place coin in pocket on right side.

*16.
A. Refold left side in.
B. Refold right side in, inserting corner of right flap into corner pocket of left flap to lock sides together and coin in place.

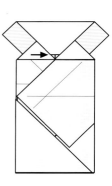

17. Mtn. fold pt. of chin under as shown.
Note: Set folds of head and hair with paper clips or tack down with glue when model is completed.

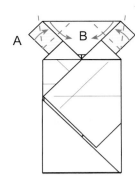

Hairstyle 1

A. Fold corners in.
Optional: Inside reverse fold corners in.
B. Fold sides in.

Result

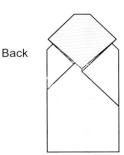

Back

Plain Paper:
Fold top edge over for bangs.

Result

Hairstyle 2

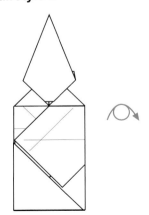

A. **Turn model over.**

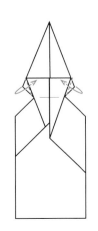

B. Fold both corners in between layers.

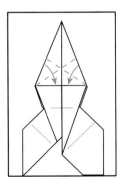

C. On both sides:
Fold each edge to folded edge. Unfold.

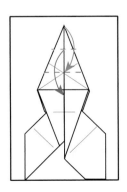

D. Fold pt. to crease intersection pt. Fold new edge down on intersection pt.

E. On both sides: Open layers and inside reverse fold corner in on creases.

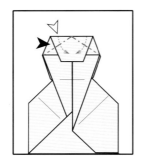 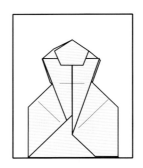 

Front

Optional Folded Fan

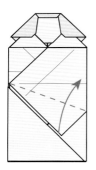

A. Fold edge up.

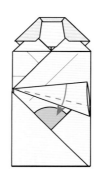

B. Fold edge down.

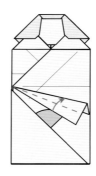

C. Fold edge up to edge.

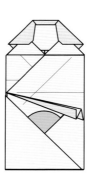

Chinese Lion

Manned by several individuals, the Chinese lion dances on Chinese New Year to ward off evil spirits. The colorful and magnificent lion dances to the beat of drums and gongs, amidst the roar of fireworks. As it parades through the streets and crowds, offerings are placed in the lion's mouth to insure a prosperous new year.

Use the specially designed Lion paper, or origami paper 15 X 15 cm. The Chinese Lion is a two-dimensional model, 2 X 3 inches. **Note:** The following instructions are for use with both the special Lion paper and plain paper. Separate instructions are clearly labeled **Lion Paper** or **Plain Paper**. Shared instructions are not labeled. See "Using the Enclosed Paper" on page 8.

1. Begin with desired side or lion design side down. Fold in half; unfold. Repeat.

2. Fold edge to center.

3. Fold edge to edge. Unfold completely. Repeat steps 2 and 3 on remaining 3 sides.

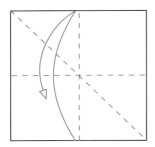

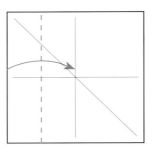

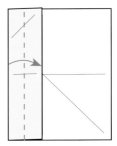

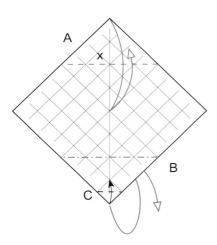

4. Rotate paper as shown.
Lion Paper: Place X as shown.
 A. Fold pt. to center. Unfold.
*B. Mtn. fold pt. behind to center. Unfold.
*C. Fold pt. to intersection pt. of creases.

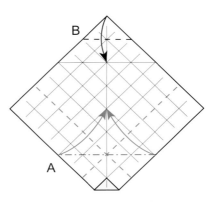

5.
*A. On creases:
 Fold edge pts. in to center.
 Flatten flap down.
 B. Fold pt. to intersection
 pt. of creases.

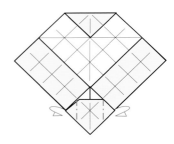

*6. Mtn. fold corners behind.

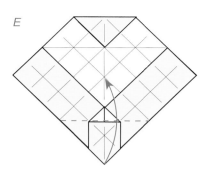

E

7. Fold pt. to intersection pt. of creases.

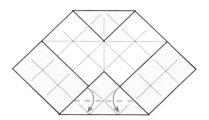

*8. Fold edges to creases.

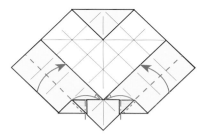

*9. Lift flap to mtn. fold corner pts. behind to center of flap, folding sides in.

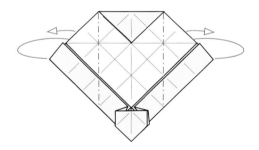

10. Mtn. fold pt. behind on intersection pt. of creases. Unfold.

*11. Open between flaps 1 and 2. On creases: Fold crease pt. to center, folding side in.

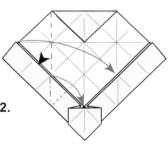

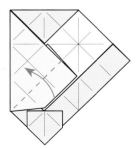

12. Fold edge to crease.

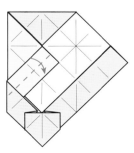

*13. Fold edge to edge.

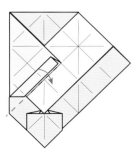

*14. Fold flap down.

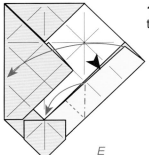

15. Repeat steps 11 (shown) through 14 on the right.

E

*16. Fold edge to crease. Model becomes three-dimensional as top and right sections are raised.

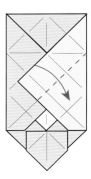

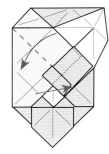

17.
A. Lift left flap over right.
*B. Fold edge to crease.

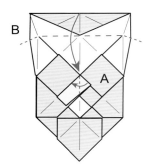

B

A

18.
A. Fold edge to edge. **Unfold.**
*B. Fold section flat on creases.

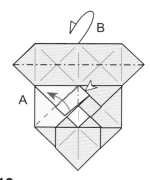

B

A

19.
A. Fold open on crease. Flatten section on creases.
B. Mtn. fold edge behind.

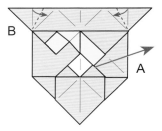

E

B

A

20.
A. Lift right flap over left. Repeat steps 18A and 19A on right.
*B. Fold crease to crease on both sides.

Insert coin in mouth pocket and under flaps.

21. Mtn. fold corners behind, raising ears.

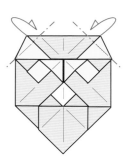

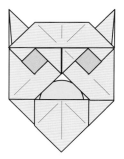

Shave Ice

A popular island treat is a cone full of finely shaved ice in a rainbow of flavors and colors. Sweet and cool, a shave ice is one of life's simple pleasures, especially on hot day.

Use the specially designed Shave Ice paper, or origami paper 15 X 15 cm. The Shave Ice is a two-dimensional model, 1.5 X 3.5 inches. **Note:** The following instructions are for use with both the special Shave Ice paper and plain paper. Separate instructions are clearly labeled **Shave Ice Paper** or **Plain Paper**. Shared instructions are not labeled. See "Using the Enclosed Paper" on page 8.

1. Begin with desired side down or place X on **Shave Ice Paper** as shown. Fold in half; unfold. Repeat.

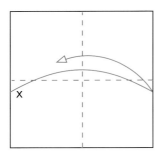

2. Mtn. fold edge to center.

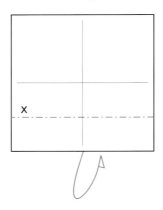

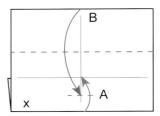

3.
Shave Ice Paper:
Skip step A.
B. Fold edge to line 3.

Plain Paper:
A. Align edge on crease. Press finger-width crease. Unfold.
B. Fold edge to new crease.

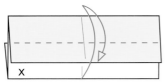

4. Fold edge up on hidden crease. Unfold edge only.

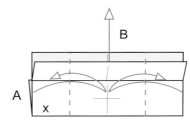

5.
A. Fold edges to center; unfold.
B. Unfold top flaps.

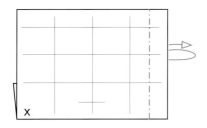

*6. Turn model over and fold edge to crease. Unfold.

*7. Rabbit ear fold flap.
Fold corner in half, refolding edges in. Mtn. fold is made by folding flap down.

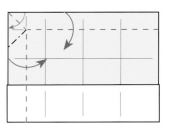

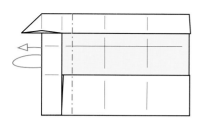

*8. Turn model over and fold edge to crease. Unfold.

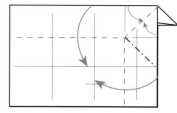

*9. Rabbit ear fold flap.
Fold corner in half, refolding edges in.
Mtn. fold is made by folding flap down.

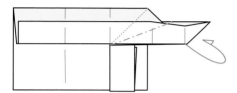

10. Mtn. fold edge under to crease.

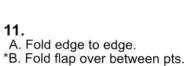

11.
 A. Fold edge to edge.
 *B. Fold flap over between pts.

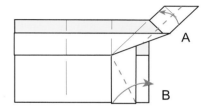

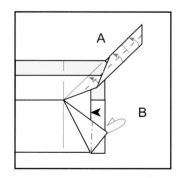

12.
A. Fold edge evenly up to edge and crease.
B. Open pocket to mtn. fold edge in behind.

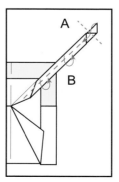

13.
A. Open layers to fold pt. under edge.
B. Fold sides up but not together to round straw.

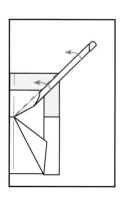

14. Fold straw over.

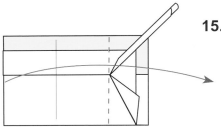

15. Fold flap over on crease.

E

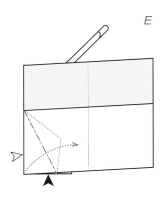

*16. Inside reverse fold corner in.
1. Establish creases:
Fold corner up between pts. Use bottom pt. of fold beneath as guide.
2. Open sides to fold corner in on creases.

B

E

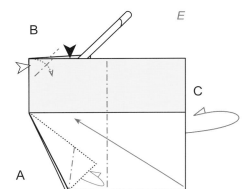

C

A

17.
A. Lift side to mtn. fold edge of inside flap behind as in step 12B.
B. Inside reverse fold corner in.
1. Establish crease:
Symmetrically fold corner down. Unfold.
2. Open layers to fold corner in on crease.
C. Mtn. fold flap behind on crease.

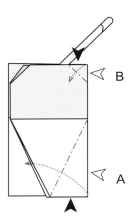

B

A

18.
*A. Inside reverse fold corner in.
(Follow step 16.)
B. Inside reverse fold corner in.
(Follow step 17B.)

A

C

B

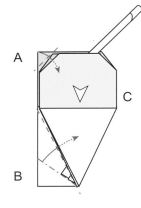

19.
A. Fold flap into pocket.
*B. Fold flap into pocket.
Flap is folded in half in process.
C. Push on edge to round.

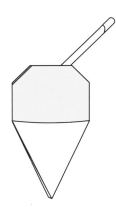

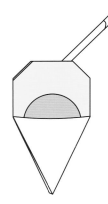

Pineapple *Hala Kahiki*

The pineapple, which is a native to South America, had been the symbol of hospitality long before it was cultivated in Hawai'i. It is appropriate, though only by coincidence, that the pineapple should also represent Hawai'i, the Land of Aloha, recognized for its friendliness and hospitality.

Use the specially designed Pineapple paper, or origami paper 15 X 15 cm. The Pineapple displays both sides of the paper. Select origami paper with sides of contrasting colors other than white. The Pineapple is a two-dimensional model, 1.5 X 2.25 inches. **Note:** The following instructions are for use with both the special Pineapple paper and plain paper. Separate instructions are clearly labeled **Pineapple Paper** or **Plain Paper**. Shared instructions are not labeled. See "Using the Enclosed Paper" on page 8. Glue is suggested. The letter G is used in the diagrams to show you where to glue. The Pineapple instructions include an optional window that requires a pair of scissors.

1. Begin with color/side for leaves down or place X on **Pineapple Paper** as shown. Fold in half; unfold. Repeat.

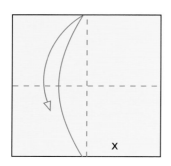

2. Fold edge to center; unfold.

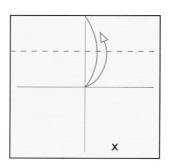

*3. Fold edge to crease.

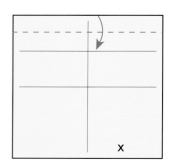

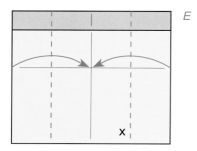

*4. Fold edges to center.

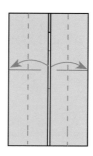

*5. Fold edges to edges.

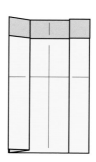

6. Turn model over.

*7. Fold edge to crease.

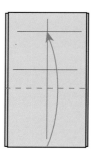

Turn model over.

Optional: To cut a window in your model follow steps A through E.

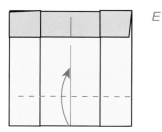

E

A. Fold edge up on crease.

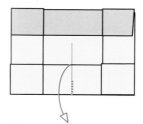

B.
Pineapple Paper:
Cut on line B. Unfold flap.
Plain Paper:
Measure, mark, and cut halfway up width of section on crease. Unfold flap.

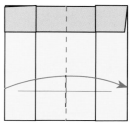

C. Fold in half.

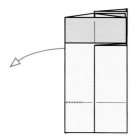

D.
Pineapple Paper:
Cut on line D. Unfold flap from behind.
Plain Paper:
Measure, mark, and cut halfway across section on crease. Unfold flap from behind.

*E. Fold each cut corner out.

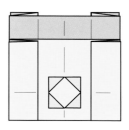

Continue with instructions.

8. Fold edges in to center.

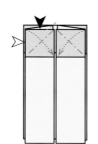

9. Inside reverse fold each corner.
1. Establish crease:
Fold corner to center; unfold.
2. Open sides to fold corner in on creases.

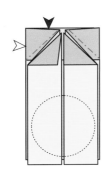

10. Inside reverse fold corners on back flaps. (Follow step 9.)

Open side to place coin in model near bottom edge.

***11.** Fold corners up as shown on right. Glue to hold.

Turn model over.

E

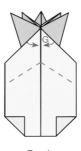

***12.** Fold corners to center.

***13.** Fold sides behind. Glue to hold near top on back.

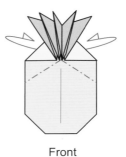

Front

Back

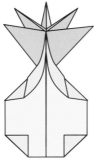

Back

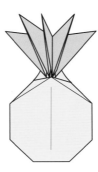

Front
(without window)

Front
(with window)

Gourd Rattle *ʻUliʻuli*

The ʻulīʻulī or gourd rattle, is a hula implement. It is made from the dried hollow fruit of the laʻamia *tree, in which seeds are placed. A handle is attached to the gourd and to that, a disk decorated with feathers and/or* kapa *cloth. The feathers are often bright red and yellow. The ʻulīʻulī is usually quickly shaken, producing a distinctive rattling sound.*

Use origami paper 15 X 15 cm to fold a model 1.5 X 1.5 inches. The Gourd Rattle is a three-dimensional model. The base of the Gourd Rattle can be purchased at a craft or hula supply store.

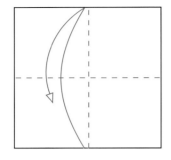

1. Begin with the desired side down. Fold in half; unfold. Repeat.

2. Fold each corner to center.

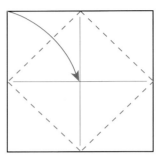

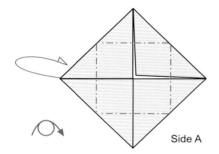

Side A

Note: Sides are now labeled A and B.

3. Turn model over to side B and fold each corner to center.

4. Fold each corner to center.

E

Side B

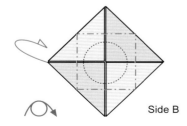

Side B

Unfold flap to slip coin under flaps beneath. Center coin. Refold.

5. Turn model over to side A and fold each corner to center.

6. Fold each corner pt. out. Set folds well.

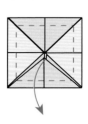

Side A

E

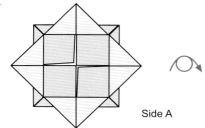

Side A

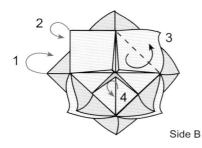

Side B

Optional: Attach base of 'ulī'ulī under center flaps.

7. **Turn model over** to side B.

8. Use the thin end of a chopstick to curl feathers.
1. Round out all bottom feathers, bending them down.
2. Curl ends under on second set of feathers.
3. Curl third set of feathers up and out.
4. Curl last set of feathers up.

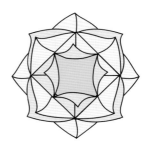

Turtle   *Honu*

From birth, the little sea turtle has many enemies. If and when it reaches adulthood, it will have but a few enemies and its chances for a very long life will be great. Thus, the turtle, honu *in Hawaiian and* kame *in Japanese, stands for endurance, longevity, and luck. It is also an image of peace, emanating a meditative calm in the roughest of seas.*

Ideally, use paper 5 inches square to fold a model 2.5 X 2.25 inches. You may also use origami paper 15 X 15 cm. The Turtle is a three-dimensional model that can be presented in two-dimensional form.

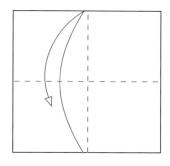

1. Begin with desired side down. Fold in half; unfold. Repeat.

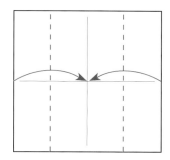

2. Fold edges to center.

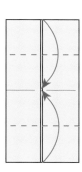

3. Fold edges to center.

E

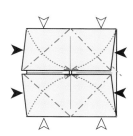

4. Inside reverse fold all corners.
1. Establish creases:
Fold corners to center. Unfold.
2. Open sides to fold corners in on creases.

E

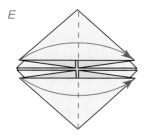

5. Fold top flaps to right.

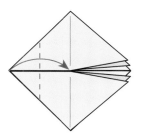

6. Fold corner pt. to center.

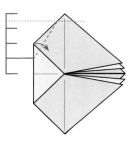

7. Fold edge in.

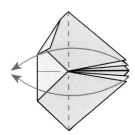

8. Fold center flaps to left. Repeat steps 6 and 7 on right flap.

Slip coin in beneath all top layers.

9. Redistribute flaps evenly.
A. Fold top pt. to center.
B. Fold pts. of flaps down.

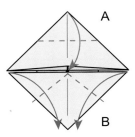

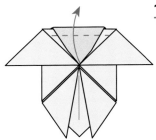

10. Fold head up.
Turn model over.

11.
A. Curl edges under.
B. Open layers of head.

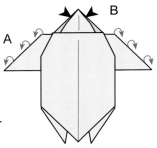

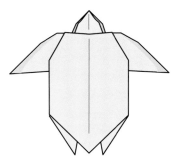

Fortune Cookie

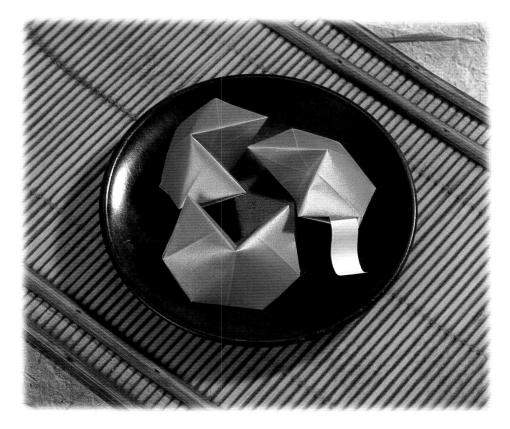

The fortune cookie reveals your destiny, and is often served after a Chinese meal. It is rumored that the message-bearing cookie was invented by an American. This is supported by the fact that the majority of cookies consumed in Hawai'i are either baked fresh in the islands or imported not from China but from Queens, New York.

Use origami paper 15 X 15 cm or 17.5 X 17.5 cm to fold models 1.75 X 2 inches or 2 X 2.25 inches respectively. The Fortune Cookie is a three-dimensional model. Place slips of paper with written fortunes in cookies instead of coins.

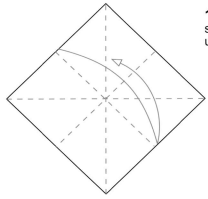

1. Begin with desired side down. Fold in half; unfold. Repeat.

2. Fold each corner to center.

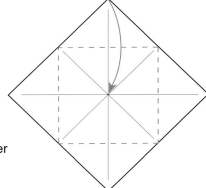

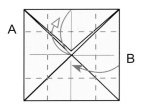

Optional: Glue or tape corners down at center.

3.
A. Fold edges to center. Unfold.
B. Fold edges to center.

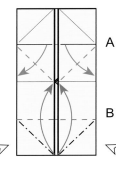

4.
A. Fold creases on to edges.
B. On creases:
Fold corner pts. to center.
Push to flatten edges.

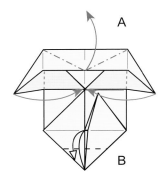

5.
A. Fold corner pts. to center, folding center pt. of edge up.
B. Fold pt. to crease; unfold.

6.
A. Fold pt. to crease; unfold.
B. Fold flaps up.
C. Open sides to invert pt. on creases.

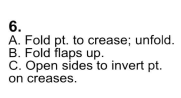

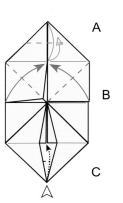

A

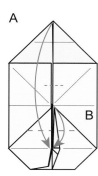

7.
A. Align pt. on crease. Press finger-width crease. Unfold.
B. Fold flaps down.

B

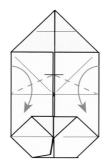

8. On both sides: Establish crease between crease pts. **Unfold.**

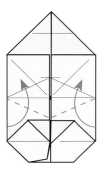

9. On both sides: Establish crease between crease pt. and inner corner pts. of flaps. **Unfold.**

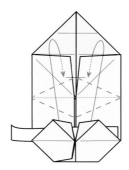

Place fortune under lower flaps as shown.

10. Fold sides together, inserting flaps into pockets.

11.
A. Mtn. fold tab into pocket.
B. Pinch sides closer together.
C. Insert toothpick into sides to round model from inside.

B

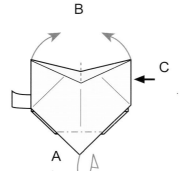

C

A

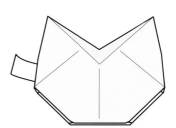

Rabbit *Lāpaki*

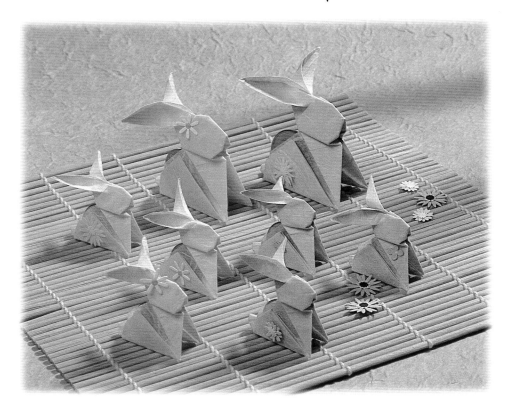

In Hawai'i, wild rabbits exist on the two small islands of Lehua and Mānana or Rabbit Island. Introduced later by the Europeans, and exiled onto uninhabited islands, the rabbit had no part in Hawaiian culture. The rabbit in local culture today is recognized as a Chinese astrological sign and, of course, as the ever-popular Easter bunny. Rabbits symbolize spring, renewal, fertility, and continuance, and they have at least one lucky foot.

Use origami paper 15 X 15 cm to fold a model 1.75 X 2.5 inches. The Rabbit is a three-dimensional model that can be presented in two-dimensional form.

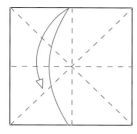

1. Begin with desired side down.
Fold in half; unfold. Repeat.

2. Fold edges to center. Unfold.

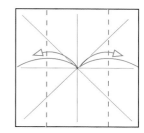

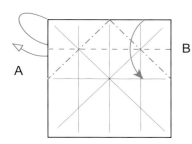

3.
A. Mtn. fold corners behind to center; unfold.
B. Fold edge to center.

4. On both sides and on creases:
Fold edge pt. to center.
Fold side in on crease.
Mtn. fold corner in half.

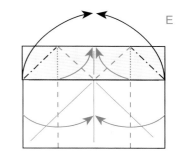

5.
A. Fold each edge in between pt. and crease pt. Fold edges in as close to center as possible.
B. Mtn. fold edge behind to center.

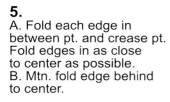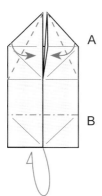

6.
A. Rabbit ear fold.
1. Establish creases:
Fold each edge to edge. Unfold.
2. Refold sides in as you (B) mtn. fold model in half on vertical center crease.

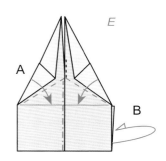

7. Rotate model as shown.
Fold head down between crease pt. and top edge of body.

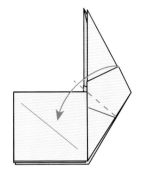

E

8. Fold head up.

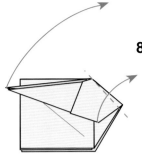

9.
A. Fold edge over. Fold is partially made beneath layer of head.
B. Fold corner up. Repeat B fold

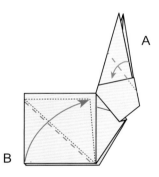

A

B

10. Rotate model as shown.
A. Unhook pleat. Redirect creases to mirror pleat creases of other side.
B. Open sides to inside reverse fold corner in.

E

A

B

11.
A. Open sides of head to reverse fold corner in.
B. Open sides to reverse fold corner out.
C. Push to reverse fold corners in.

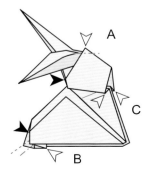

A

C

B

Slip coin in between open layers on back.

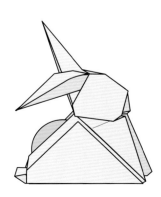

Rooster *Moa Kāne*

The rooster is bestowed with many virtues. To the Portuguese, he symbolizes luck, faith, and justice. The Chinese attribute the rooster with civility, generosity, reliability, and valor. It is believed that symbolically the rooster chases away evil spirits because he crows at first light.

Use origami paper 17.5 X 17.5 cm to fold a model 2.75 X 2.5 inches. The Rooster is a three-dimensional model that can be presented in near two-dimensional form. Use origami paper 15 X 15 cm to fold a model of a size more suitable for quarters.

1. Begin with desired side up.
Fold in half; unfold. Repeat.

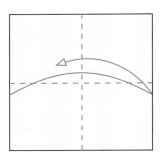

2. Fold edges to center.

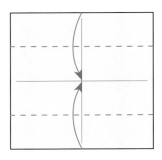

3. Fold edges to edges.

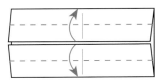

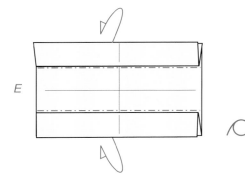

4. Turn model over
and fold edges to center.

5.
A. Inside reverse fold corners of all four flaps on right.
1. Establish creases:
Fold corner to center; unfold.
2. Open sides to fold corner in on creases.
B. Mtn. fold corners of both flaps to center.
C. Fold corners of flaps to center.

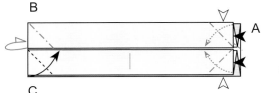

6. Fold edge up to center.

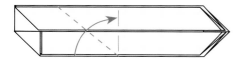

7. Rabbit ear fold.
1. Establish creases:
Fold edge to edge. (See 7a.) Crease only as shown.
Unfold. Repeat on opposite edge.
2. Refold edges up on creases as you fold sides together.
3. Mtn. fold is made by folding new flap up.

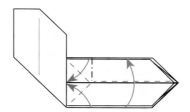

7a.

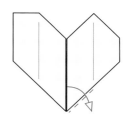

A

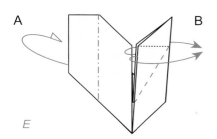

B

E

8.
A. Mtn. fold edge behind on crease.
B. Outside reverse fold flap.
1. Establish creases between pts. *Note edge of hidden layer.*
2. Partially unfold rabbit ear fold.
3. Fold sides out on creases. (See 8a.)
4. Refold completely.

8a.

Place coin in model as shown.

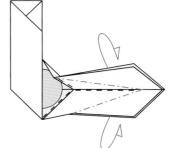

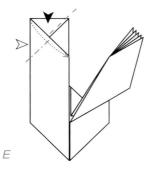

9. Inside reverse fold corner.
1. Open sides.
2. Fold corner in. Use folded edge as guide.

E

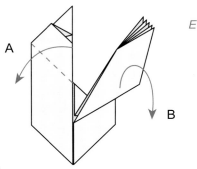

E

10.
A. Fold section down between pts.
B. Bend tail over.

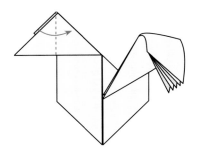

11. Fold edges of both flaps to edge.

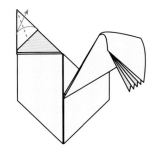

12. Fold edge to edge. Lift flap perpendicular on crease.

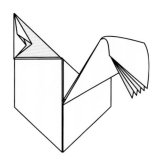

13. Turn model over.

14.
A. Fold pt. down at angle.
B. Curl flaps.

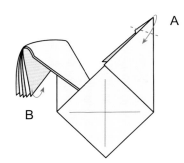

15.
A. Pinch sides of bottom corner together to mtn. fold.
B. Shape model by bending edges behind.

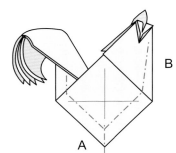

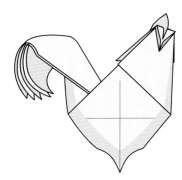

Coin Frame

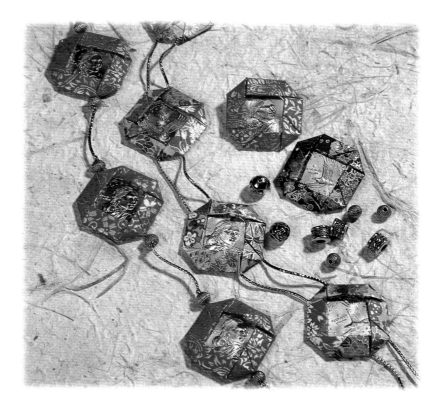

The Coin Frame is a special envelope that displays
individual coins. The Coin Frame accentuates a coin
with added color and frames the intricate artwork
that is embossed on each piece.

Use origami paper 7.5 X 7.5 cm to frame gold dollars. Paper 2.75 inches square, which must be cut, creates a Coin Frame that fits a little more snugly around the dollar coin and is more suitable for directly stringing into leis. When using paper of this size, the coin is slipped into the frame after step 10. The Coin Frame is a two-dimensional model 1.5 X 1.5 inches. Use paper 2.5 inches square to frame quarters. Instructions on how to string coin frames into a lei follow general model instructions.

1. Begin with desired side down. Fold in half. Unfold.

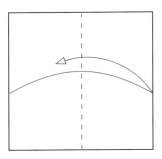

2. Fold edges to center.

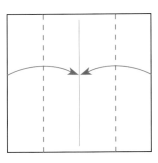

3. Fold in half.

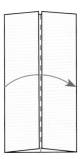

4. Fold each side in half. Unfold completely.

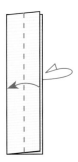

5. Rotate paper as shown. Repeat steps 1 (shown) through 4.

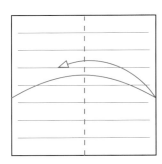

6. On creases:
A. Fold edge to crease.
B. Fold new edge to crease.
Note center square.

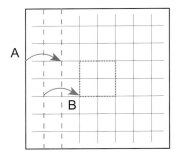

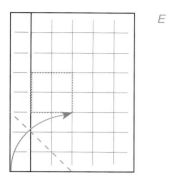

E

7. Fold corner pt. to corner pt. of center square.

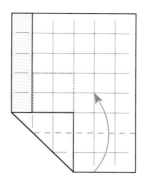

8. Fold edge to crease.

9. Open layers to mtn. fold edge behind.

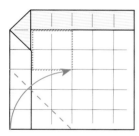

10. Rotate paper as shown.
Repeat steps 7 (shown) through 9.

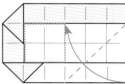

11. Fold corner pt. to corner pt. of center square.

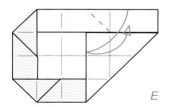

E

12. Fold edge to edge. Crease only as shown. Unfold.

13. Separate top layer. Fold crease pt. to crease pt.

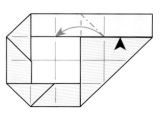

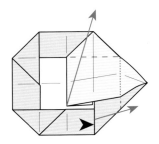

14. Lift sides perpendicular.

15. Mtn. fold edge down on crease. Edge is partly folded over indicated lifted flap.

Slip coin in frame.

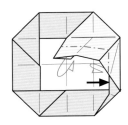

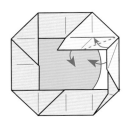

16. Fold edge to crease as you fold sides down.

17. Lift side to mtn. fold pt. under to indicated corner pt.

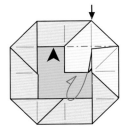

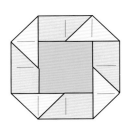

Lei:
Complete Frames up through step 15, without inserting coins. String Frames together. Tape thread, yarn, etc. to inside of frame or knot at sides if spaces are left between frames. Place coins in finished lei. Glue final fold in place to secure coin.

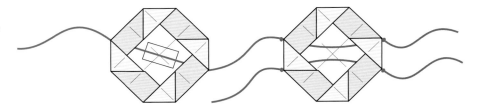

Lucky Frog *Poloka*

Kaeru *means "frog" in Japanese. The same word also means "to return." The lucky frog is based on the idea that what is contributed will return tenfold. To be considered lucky, the frog must be received as a gift and it must have an open mouth in which to accept fortune.*

Ideally, use paper 5 inches square to fold a model 2 X 2.25 inches. Otherwise, use origami paper 15 X 15 cm to fold a model 2.25 X 2.5 inches. The Lucky Frog is a three-dimensional model that can be presented in two-dimensional form.

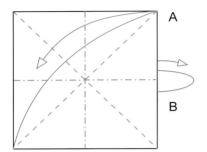

A

B

1. Begin with desired side down.
A. Fold in half; unfold. Repeat.
B. Mtn. fold in half; unfold. Repeat.

2. Fold corners to center; unfold.

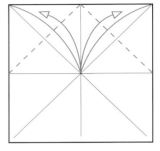

3. Fold edge pts. down and in to center.

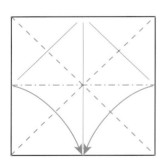

3a.

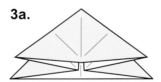

4. Fold center pt. of edge to pt. and edges to center.

E

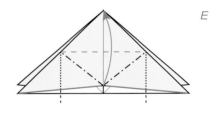

5. On both sides:
Fold corner pt. up to pt.
Flatten edge on creases.

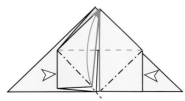

6. Fold flap over.

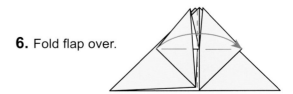

7. Fold pt. to center.
Note: Align pt. on edge beneath.

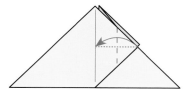

8. Fold edge in between pts. shown.

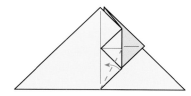

9. Fold flaps over.
Repeat steps 7 through 9 on right.

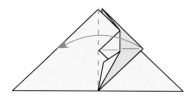

10. Squash fold both sides.
1. Establish crease:
Fold flap in half. Lift section perpendicular.
2. Open layers.
3. Push edge down flattening section symmetrically.

E

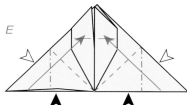
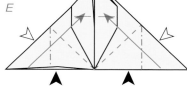

11. Petal fold both sides.
1. Establish creases as seen on left side:
Fold edges to center of flap. Unfold.
2. Fold pt. up. between crease pts.
3. Fold edges in. Gently stretch flap to align edges on center line.

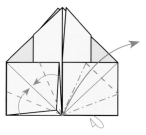

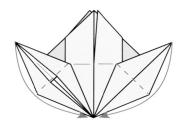

12. Fold flaps down.

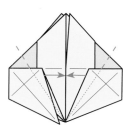

13. Fold edges of flaps to center.

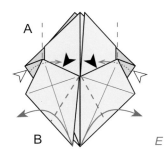

14.
A. On both sides:
Open layers to inside reverse
fold section in against edge
of body.
B. Fold pts. of flaps up and out.

15.
A. Fold pts. of flaps straight out.
B. Fold pt. up.

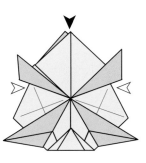

16. On both sides:
Fold edge to edge.

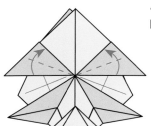

17. To give frog dimension:
A. Partly open mouth.
B. Push in on sides of frog's body
   (not legs) to slightly round back.
   Turn model over.

Place coin in mouth.
Optional: Use double-stick tape
to hold coin in place.

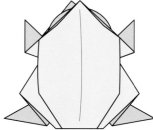

Flower Coin Purse

The Flower Coin Purse secures your gift within a swirl of petals.
The purse is opened by simply pulling on opposing petals and
closed, by pushing them back to center. The gift coin is
contained and hidden below within a special compartment.

Ideally, use paper 4.5 inches square to fold a model 2.25 X 2.25 inches. You may also use origami paper 15 X 15 cm to fold a model 3 X 3 inches. The Flower Coin Purse is primarily a two-dimensional model. Instructions are provided for a petal variation.

1. Begin with desired side down. Fold in half; unfold. Repeat.

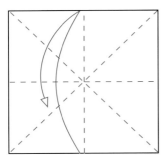

2. Fold each corner to center. *Optional: Glue or tape corners at center.*

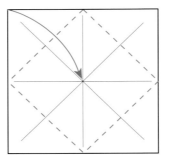

3. Mtn. fold and unfold each edge to center.

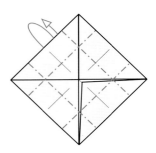

Step 4 is optional. It creates creases to help accurately fold steps 7 and 9.

E

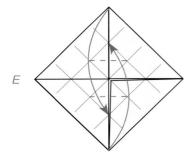

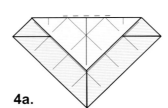

4a.

4. Touch pt. to crease intersection pt. Crease as shown. (See 4a.) Unfold. Repeat.

Note position of step 4 creases.

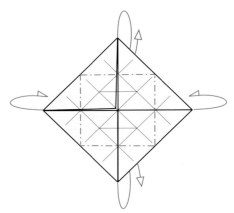

5. Mtn. fold each pt. behind to center. Unfold top and bottom flaps.

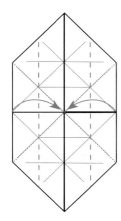

E

6. Fold edge to center and flaps up from behind.

7. Fold pts. out and down to corner pts. as you fold top pt. down to pt.

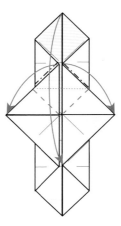

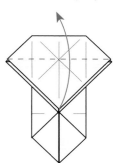

8. Fold flap up.

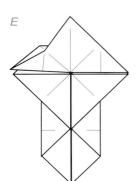

E

9. Repeat steps 7 and 8 on lower half.

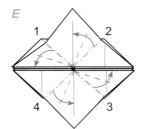

E

10. Pleat fold in order. Raise crease into edge. Fold new edge over.

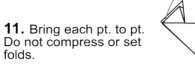

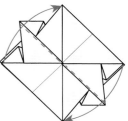

11. Bring each pt. to pt. Do not compress or set folds.

12. Pleat fold in order. Raise crease into edge. Fold new edge over.

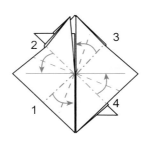

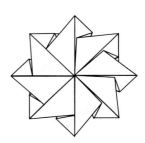

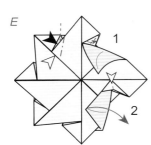

E

13. Inside reverse fold all corners:
1. Bend petal up to open layers. Fold edge to edge.
2. Push crease in. Return petal. Fold edge of petal to match edge beneath (fold 1).

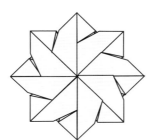

Gently pull opposing petals away from center to open model.

Place coin in center.

Push petals back in place to close model.

Petal Variation:
Reverse direction of overlapped sections. Leave as is or lift sections perpendicular on creases.

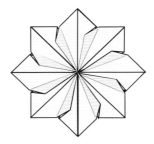

Dolphin *Nai'a*

Nai'a, *which also means "porpoise," refers to the four species of dolphins found in island waters. Altogether, there are thirty-one species of dolphins in the world. The dolphin has many admirable qualities. It is playful, sociable, compassionate, and highly intelligent. Physically, the dolphin is sleek, fast, and powerful.*

Use origami paper 11 X 11 cm (approximately 4.25 inches square) to fold a model 2 X 2.25 inches, in which to hold a gold dollar. Quarters require paper 4 inches square. The Dolphin is a three-dimensional model that can be presented in two-dimensional form. Use paper backed origami foil to create beautiful but fragile models with sculpted detail.

1. Begin with desired side down.
A. Fold in half; unfold. Repeat.
B. Mtn. fold in half; unfold.

2. Fold edges to center.

3. Mtn. fold edge behind to center. Unfold completely.

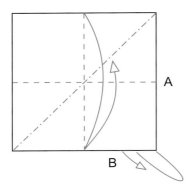

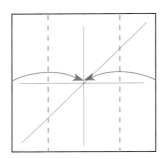

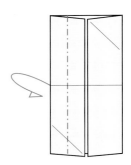

4. Fold edges to center; unfold.

6. Fold edges to creases.

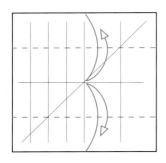

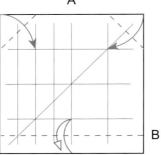

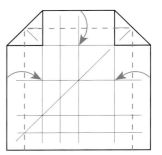

5.
A. Fold corners to creases.
B. Fold edge to crease; unfold.

E

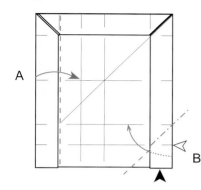

7.
A. Fold edge to crease.
B. Inside reverse fold.
1. Establish creases:
Fold edge to crease. Unfold.
2. Open sides to fold edge
in on creases.

A

B

8. Refold to freshen required
creases. Fold corner pt. and
edge pt. in together.

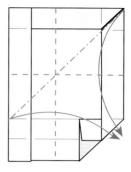

9. Rotate model as shown.
Fold edge to crease.
Optional: Unfold. Sink fold pt. in on creases.
Note: Sink folding is not necessary when
using foil-based paper or glue.

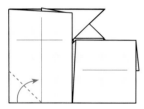

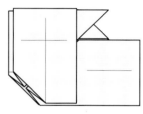

Sink Fold Result

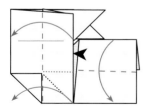

10. Fold edge to edge, folding pt. over.
Fold edge to edge. Flatten to set fold.

11.
A. Fold edge up between pts.
B. & C. Squash fold.
1. Lift corner of flap on crease.
2. Open between first and second layers.
3. Push on edge. Flatten symmetrically.
D. Fold corner behind between layers or
fold into optional sink fold.

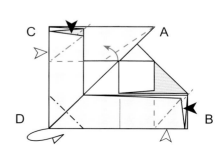

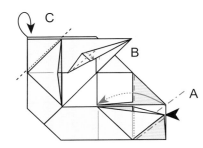

12.
A. Open tail layers to fold on crease pt. to pt. under white flap.
B. Fold edge to edge.
C. Fold back corner between layers.

Place coin under body layer and under both tail layers.

13.
A. Flip tail to back.
B. Fold pt. up to crease pt.

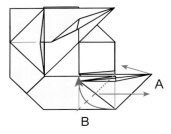

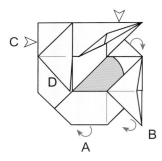

14.
A. Round edges back.
B. Lift tail fin. Slightly curl down.
C. Push on edge of head and of dorsal fin to indent.
D. Lift pectoral fin slightly.

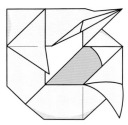

Nesting Crane *Manu ʻū*

The crane is revered as a symbol of perseverance and longevity. It is said to live a thousand years. This is the premise of the Japanese custom of folding a thousand cranes for luck. In Hawaiʻi, it is a local custom to add another crane, making it a thousand and one.

Use origami paper 15 X 15 cm preferably with a color pattern in which the corners of the paper vary in color from its center. The Nesting Crane is either a two- or three-dimensional model, 1.75 X 1.75 inches.

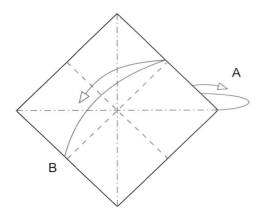

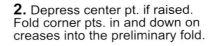

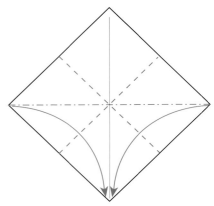

1. Begin with desired side down.
A. Mtn. fold in half; unfold. Repeat.
B. Fold in half; unfold. Repeat.

2. Depress center pt. if raised. Fold corner pts. in and down on creases into the preliminary fold.

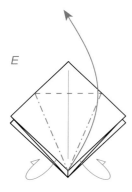

E

3. Petal fold.
1. Establish creases:
Fold edges to center. (See 3a.) Unfold.
2. Fold flap up between crease pts.
3. Fold edges in. Gently stretch to align on center. (See 3b.)
Repeat petal fold behind.

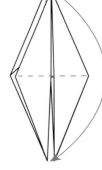
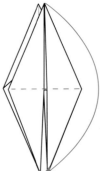

4. Fold flap down. Repeat behind.

3a.

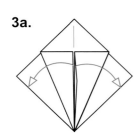

3b.

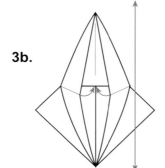

5. Precrease all layers.
1. Fold pt. down.
2. Fold behind on same crease.
Unfold model completely.

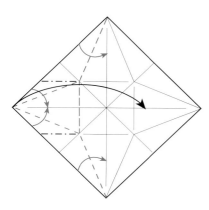

6. *Note: All creases except mtn. folds are existing.*
Fold edges in and side flap up. Fold edges
of flap in while folding flap down, aligning
pt. on center line. Mtn. folds are made in
the process. Set folds well.

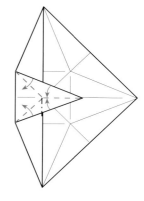

7. Rabbit ear fold flap.
Pinch/fold flap in half to base, folding edges
over in the process. Fold flap up then down.
Repeat steps 6 and 7 on the right.

E

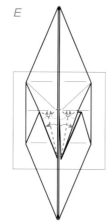

8. Rabbit ear fold both sides:
Pinch/fold flap in half to base,
folding edges to horizontal
center line.

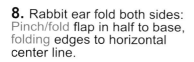

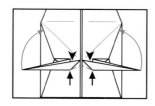

9. On both sides:
Slightly open layers.
Pivot flap up on indicated
pt. Align pt. on inner
edge. Set new fold.

10. Rabbit ear fold flap.
1. Establish each crease:
Fold edge to center line.
(See 10a.) Crease as shown.
Unfold.
2. Refold edges to center
while folding flap in half.
3. Fold flap over to left.

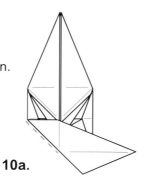

10a.

*Slip coin under top layers
and place near bottom of
model.*

11. Repeat rabbit ear fold
but fold edges under head
and tail flaps.

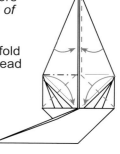

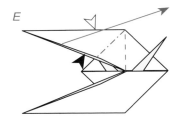

E

12. Squash fold.
1. Establish:
Fold flap to right. Unfold.
2. *Optional: Establish creases:*
Fold top edge of flap to crease. Unfold.
3. Lift flap perpendicular.
4. Open layers.
5. Push edge down to flatten section
symmetrically on creases

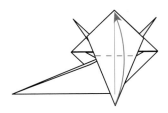

13. Fold flap in half
to pt.

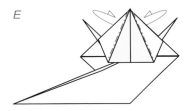

E

14. Mtn. fold edges
behind to center.

15. Inside reverse fold each corner.
1. Establish creases:
Fold corner to center; unfold.
2. Open sides to fold corner in on
creases.

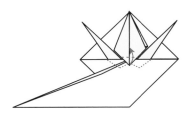

16.
A. Fold pt. up as far
as possible.
B. Lift lower edges of
head and tail flaps
over top layer.

17. Repeat steps 12 (shown)
through 15 on lower flap.

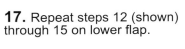

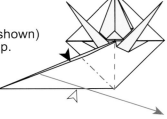

18.
A. Outside reverse fold head:
Open sides of flap to fold
sides of tip out and down.
B. Insert pt. of lower wing into
pocket of wing above.

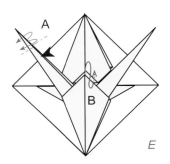

A

B

E

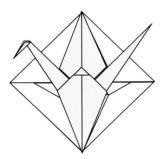

Bat *Ōpe'ape'a*

The Hawaiian hoary bat is one of only two land mammals that are native to Hawai'i. It lives in trees and is mainly found on Kaua'i, Maui, and the Big Island. It weighs a mere half ounce at the most and has a wingspan that reaches a little over a foot.

Use origami paper 15 X 15 cm to fold a model 2 X 2 inches. The Bat is a three-dimensional model that can be presented in two-dimensional form.

1. Begin with desired side down. Fold in half; unfold. Repeat.

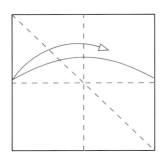

2. Fold edge to center.

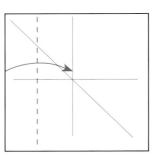

3. Mtn. fold edge behind to center. Unfold completely.

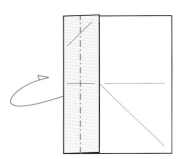

4. Fold edge to center. Repeat steps 2 and 3.

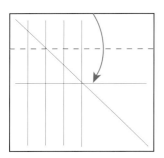

5.
A. Mtn. fold corner behind to center; unfold.
B. Fold corner to center.

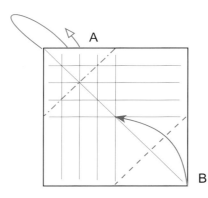

6. Rotate paper as shown. Fold edge pts. to center on creases.

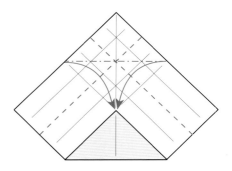

E

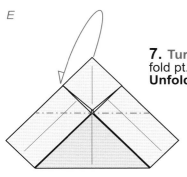

7. Turn paper over and fold pt. to bottom edge. **Unfold.**

8. On each side: Align edge on crease. Crease only as shown. (See 8a.) **Unfold.**

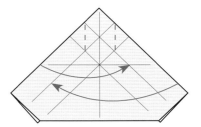

8a.

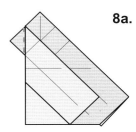

9. *Note: All creases are existing except* *valley fold.*
1. Raise sides on creases.
2. Fold edge pts. in to center.
3. Fold pt. down on center line.

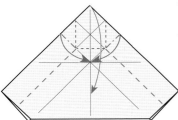

10. Inside reverse fold each corner.
1. Establish creases:
Fold corner to center; unfold.
2. Open sides to fold corner in on creases.

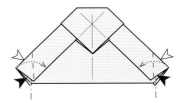

E

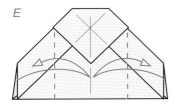

11. Fold edges to center. Unfold. **Turn model over.**

12. Fold pts. up to center. Unfold.

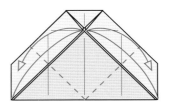

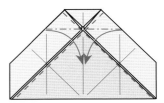

13. Fold edge pts. in to center on creases raising flap up from behind.

Bat

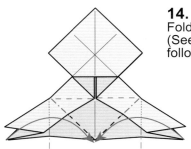

14. On creases:
Fold pts. of wings in to center.
(See fold in progress in
following step.)

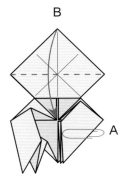

15.
A. Temporarily paperclip wing
to set folds as seen on right.
B. Fold pt. to pt.

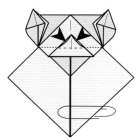

16.
A. Squash fold.
1. Lift flap perpendicular against folded edge.
2. Open layers.
3. Flatten section symmetrically.
B. Fold pt. to imaginary pt.

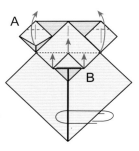

17.
A. Fold tips of ears up.
Note crease placement.
B. Fold pt. up. Align crease
on imaginary line

18. Lift flap perpendicular on crease.
Open layers, partially flattening pt.

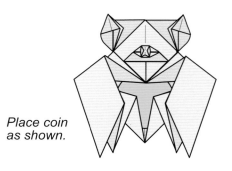

*Place coin
as shown.*

Owl   *Pueo*

*There are two species of owls in Hawai'i. One is the introduced American barn owl
and the other is the native* pueo *or short-eared brown owl. The* pueo *was present in
Hawai'i before humankind. Although endangered and amidst changes, it is still present
on all the islands, including O'ahu. The* pueo *was and still is revered in Hawai'i.*

Use origami paper 15 X 15 cm to fold a model 2 X 2.5 inches. The Owl is a slightly three-dimensional model.

Follow steps 1 through 10 of the Bat. Turn model over.

11.
A. Fold flap behind on crease.
B. Fold pt. to edge.

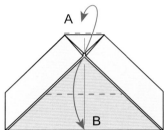

Place coin behind flap.

12. Fold edge pts. in to center on creases. Flap is raised up from behind. Flatten to set folds.

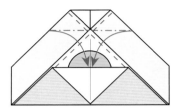

13.
A. Fold pts. to center.
B. Fold pts. to center

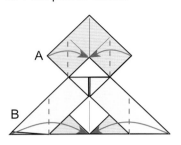

14.
A. Mtn. fold pt. behind. Unfold. *Note crease placement.*
B. Mtn. fold edges behind to center.
Optional: Temporarily set wing folds with paperclips.

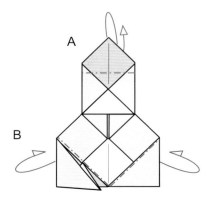

15. Separate layers. Fold edge pts. in to center. Align crease on center line. Press to hold folds on center and to hold layers open. (See 15a.) Fold pt. down on crease.

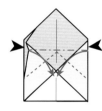

15a.

16.
A. Mtn. fold edge behind.
B. Mtn. fold pt. of top layer under.
C. Curl sides back.

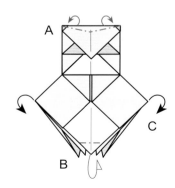

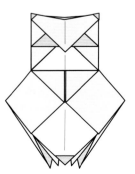

Anemone   *Ōkole Emiemi*

This model is actually a box with collapsed and pleated sides, giving it the chambered base and the flower-like appearance of a sea anemone. When a coin is locked within the chamber, the receiver is faced with a slight challenge of removing it without tearing the model.

Ideally, use paper 5 inches square to fold a model 1.5 X 1.5 inches, a suitable size for lei. You may also use origami paper 15 X 15 cm to fold a model 2.25 X 2.25 inches. The Anemone is a three-dimensional model.

Optional: Glue or tape corners at center.

1. Begin with desired side down. Fold in half; unfold. Repeat.

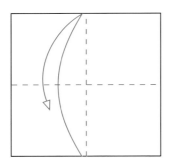

2. Fold each corner to center.

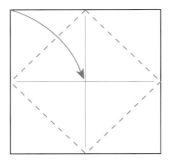

3. Turn model over and fold in half. Unfold. Repeat.

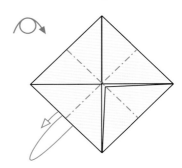

4. Fold and unfold each edge to center.

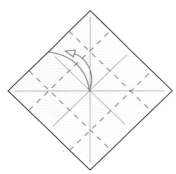

5. Fold each corner to center.

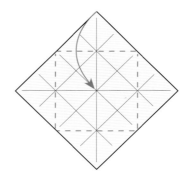

6. Fold each corner pt. to edge.

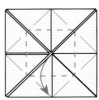

7. Unfold flaps.
Turn model over.

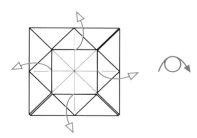

8. Fold edge to crease intersection pts. (See 8a.) Unfold. Repeat on remaining sides.

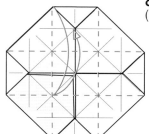

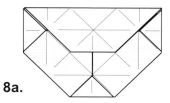

8a.

9.
A. Refold mtn. fold creases of step 3. Unfold. Do not smooth over creases.
B. Depress intersection pts.

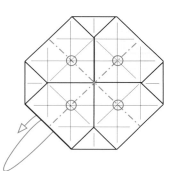

10. On both sides and on creases: Fold edge pts. to center, lifting side perpendicular. Fold flap behind.

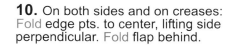

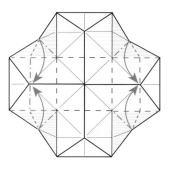

11. Fold corners of flaps to center. Repeat on opposite side.

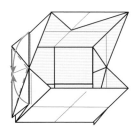

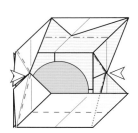

Place coin in upright model.

12. Push ends in on creases. Collapse adjacent sides in, folding flaps together at center.

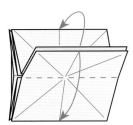

13. Fold flaps out from center on creases.

14. On each end:
Fold corners in half by pinching sides together from beneath. Pinch to set all raised edges.

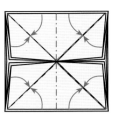

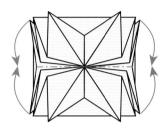

15. On both sides:
Mtn. fold flaps together. Pinch all raised edges. Evenly arrange flaps.

Lucky Lūʻau Pig *Puaʻa*

In Hawaiʻi, a child's first birthday is a special occasion often celebrated with a lūʻau *or Hawaiian feast. Traditionally, a pig is baked in an underground oven, or* imu, *and served as the main course. This sweet origami pig originally created as the Baby* Lūʻau *Pig could not be associated with such a fate so he has been granted a reprieve, thus becoming the Lucky* Lūʻau *Pig.*

Use origami paper 15 X 15 cm to fold a model 2.5 X 2.25 inches. The Pig is a three-dimensional model that can be presented in two-dimensional form.

1. Begin with desired side down. Fold in half; unfold. Repeat.

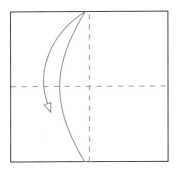

2. Fold edges to center.

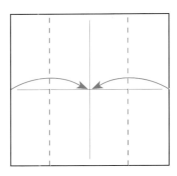

3. Fold edges to center.

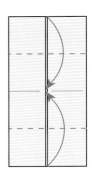

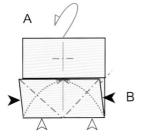

4.
A. Align edge on center line behind. Press finger-width crease. Unfold top half completely.
B. Inside reverse fold corners.
1. Establish creases:
Fold corners to center. Unfold.
2. Open sides to fold corners in on creases.

5.
A. Fold corners to center; unfold.
B. Fold pt. to edge.

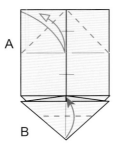

6.
A. On creases:
Lift layer. Push edge in and flatten, folding corner pt. under layer. Repeat.
B. Fold pt. of flap to edge.

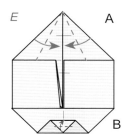

E

7.
A. Fold edges to center.
Crease only as shown.
B. Fold pt. to edge.
Crease well.

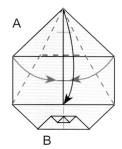

8.
A. Fold each corner pt. to crease.
Sides of flap are refolded in on
creases, raising flap up on edge.
Fold flap down.
B. Unfold lower half completely.

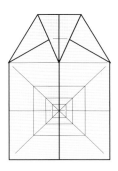

9. Turn model over.

10.
A. Fold edge only to crease, folding flap up
from behind.
B. Define and raise edges of center
square, refolding creases up to square and
refolding sides in and together.

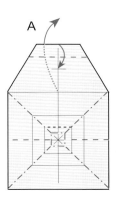

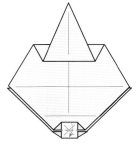

E

11.
Fold edge of square down.
Turn model over.

12.
Fold pts. of top flaps to center.

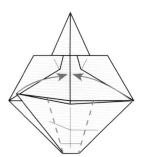

13.
Fold pts. of flaps straight out.

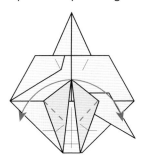

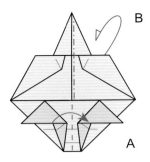

14.
A. Fold flap over to right.
B. Mtn. fold sides together.

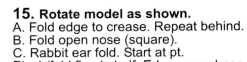

15. Rotate model as shown.
A. Fold edge to crease. Repeat behind.
B. Fold open nose (square).
C. Rabbit ear fold. Start at pt.
Pinch/fold flap in half. Edges near base
of tail are folded over in the process.
Fold flap down.

E

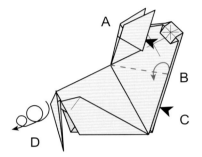

16.
A. Round open and round back ears.
B. Slightly fold head forward.
C. Slightly part front legs and sides of
top of head.
D. Curl tail.

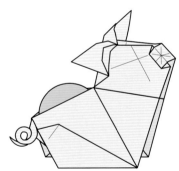

*Slip coin in between
open layers on back.*